Date: 1/23/12

If I Were a
Ballerina

by Thomas Kingsley Troupe   illustrated by Heather Heyworth

Special thanks to our advisers for their expertise:

Eryn A. Michlitsch, Artistic Director
Mankato Ballet Company

Terry Flaherty, Ph.D., Professor of English
Minnesota State University, Mankato

Picture Window Books
Minneapolis, Minnesota

Editor: Shelly Lyons
Designer: Tracy Davies
Page Production: Melissa Kes
Art Director: Nathan Gassman
Editorial Director: Nick Healy
Creative Director: Joe Ewest
The illustrations in this book were created with
traditional drawing and digital painting.

Picture Window Books
151 Good Counsel Drive
P.O. Box 669
Mankato, MN 56002-0669
877-845-8392
www.picturewindowbooks.com

Printed in the United States of America, North Mankato, Minnesota.

 All books published by Picture Window Books are manufactured with paper
containing at least 10 percent post-consumer waste.

Library of Congress Cataloging-in-Publication Data
Troupe, Thomas Kingsley.
If I were a ballerina / by Thomas Kingsley Troupe ;
illustrated by Heather Heyworth.
p. cm. — (Dream big!)
Includes index.
ISBN 978-1-4048-5532-8 (library binding)
ISBN 978-1-4048-5706-3 (paperback)
1. Ballet dancing—Juvenile literature. 2. Ballerinas—Juvenile
literature. I. Heyworth, Heather, ill. II. Title.
GV1787.5.T76 2010
792.8—dc22   2009003295

022010   005664R

If I were a ballerina, I would dance to beautiful music.

If I were a ballerina, I would wear stretchy clothing. It would let me move freely.

I would tie my
shoes tight.

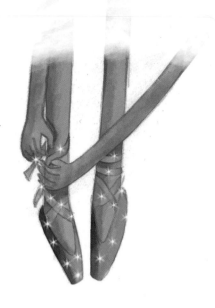

I would wrap my
hair in a bun.

After many lessons, a ballerina gets pointe
shoes. Pointe shoes help a ballerina dance
on the tips of her toes.

If I were a ballerina, I would line up with the other dancers. I would rest my ankle on the barre and stretch.

Steady on those toes!

If I were a ballerina, my muscles would work hard. I would have perfect balance. I would keep my head high and my back straight.

A ballerina does centre work. She must show good balance and form without the barre. She turns, leaps, and jumps to music.

If I were a ballerina, I would practice turnout. I would turn my hips, knees, and feet outward. This would help me stay balanced while raising a leg into the air.

FIRST POSITION

In ballet, there are five basic positions. The positions are for both the feet and arms. The positions help dancers stay balanced.

Hold it there!

If I were a ballerina, I would wait
backstage with the other dancers.
The theater would be packed. I would
love performing for a large crowd!

Shhh! It's almost time!

If I were a ballerina, I would whirl as the music began to play. I would spin on my toes. My arms would be out in front of me, in first position.

If I were a ballerina, I would let the music move me. My partner would lift me high above the stage. The audience would gasp!

A ballerina's male partner is called a *danseur*.

If I were a ballerina, I would leap across the stage. I would be a living, dancing work of art.

If I were a ballerina, I would finish my dance with a curtsey. The audience would clap and cheer for me!

How do you get to be a Ballerina?

Most ballerinas start ballet classes at a very young age. Some ballerinas take three to six lessons a week. Serious students of ballet will join a dance school. There, they learn to dance in front of an audience.

With practice, the ballerina becomes a better dancer. Soon, she can try out to join a professional ballet company. Only the best ballerinas are asked to join the company.

Many ballerinas become professionals before the age of 20. Well-trained ballerinas practice daily. The hard work is worth it. Ballet brings joy and beauty to many people!

Glossary

ballerina–a female ballet dancer

barre–a wooden rod attached to the wall at the ballerina's waist level, usually in front of a mirror

centre work–work done without the barre

curtsey–a bending of the knees and waist, like a bow at the end of a performance

danseur–a male ballet dancer

pointe shoes–hand-crafted shoes with a hard, square tip; they allow ballerinas to balance on the tips of their toes

positions–there are five basic ballet positions for both the feet and arms

professional–a person who works for money doing something that other people do for fun

turnout–when the hips, knees, and feet are turned outward; the feet are placed with the heels together and toes pointing away

To Learn More

More Books to Read

Bussell, Darcey, and Patricia Linton. *The Ballet Book*. New York: DK, 2006.

Ellison, Nancy, and Susan Jaffe. *Becoming a Ballerina*. New York: Universe Pub., distributed by St. Martin's Press, 2003.

Feldman, Jane. *We Love Ballet!* New York: Random House, 2004.

Thompson, Lauren. *Ballerina Dreams*. New York: Feiwel and Friends, 2007.

Internet Sites

FactHound offers a safe, fun way to find Internet sites related to this book. All of the sites on FactHound have been researched by our staff.

Here's all you do:

Visit *www.facthound.com*

FactHound will fetch the best sites for you!

Index

Look for all of the books in the Dream Big! series: